The Times Nature Diary

Derwent May, a nature-writer in the tradition of Gilbert White and W.H.Hudson, is also a novelist and the Literary Editor of *The Listener*. His novels include *The Laughter in Djakarta* (1973) and *A Revenger's Comedy* (1979).

Richard Blake has always been deeply interested in the British countryside. From his Surrey studio he has completed many private wildlife commissions. This book, however, marks the first major publication of this talented artist's work.

The Times Nature Diary

Derwent May

Illustrated by Richard Blake

Robson Books

FIRST PUBLISHED IN GREAT BRITAIN IN 1983 BY ROBSON BOOKS LTD., BOLSOVER HOUSE, 5-6 CLIPSTONE STREET, LONDON W1P 7EB. THIS PAPERBACK EDITION PUBLISHED IN 1984.

British Library Cataloguing in Publication Data

May, Derwent
The Times nature diary.
1. Natural History – Great Britain
I. Title
508.41 QH137

ISBN 0-86051-266-5PB
ISBN 0-86051-225-8HB

Printed in Hungary

Preface

This Nature Diary is based on the 'Nature Notes' that have been published in *The Times* every week since July 1981 — slightly erratically at first, but soon settling down as a regular Monday morning feature. They form part of a back-page panel called The Times Information Service; and their main aim is to be short bulletins on what can be seen in the countryside each week. There is usually a paragraph on birds, and another on trees, flowers and other creatures. The presence of humans in the countryside — knocking down conkers or being stung by nettles — is also sometimes evoked. About 400 species of wild life are mentioned in the Notes in the course of a year, some of them quite frequently.

From the start, however, while striving to be factual, I have always aimed to be more than merely factual. I didn't want to be sentimental about nature, or literary — but I have tried to be vivid, catching a sharp impression of a bird or a tree-shape in a few words. Often, I think, I have been helped by having so few words at my disposal: it has forced me to focus all the more clearly on the picture I want to give.

The entries cover what one might call an 'average' year in England (though I have also occasionally sent the Notes off on short forays into Scotland). But of course there is no average visible in nature. Every year the weather is different; there are differences in the progress of spring on a hilltop and in the next valley; indeed, trees of the same species may come into leaf or lose their leaves at quite different times, even in the same garden. Only the arrival of some spring birds seems marvellously constant: chiffchaffs in the last week of March, or swifts at the end of the first week in May. So I hope that readers will find part of the interest in the book in comparing their year, in their neighbourhood, with this one.

My thanks to all the readers who wrote asking if the Notes would appear in a book; and to the Editor of *The Times*, for permission to reprint them here.

D.J.M.

1 January – 7 January

ON a fine morning, crows court in the treetops: the male humps his back, bows, and spreads his tail, sometimes producing a strange, grating trill, like a football-rattle. Rooks sit about their old nests in the rookeries before setting off to feed for the day. Starlings are singing, even when the days are very bleak, a subdued song of squeaks and whirrs, though sometimes bursting into a strong musical passage. Linnets are beginning to sing again, a rather casual, twangy performance. Hedge-sparrows are in regular song, and also engage in excited, wing-flicking chases, apparently of a sexual nature. Wrens emerge from the brushwood, sing loudly, then slip back out of sight again.

Snowdrops begin to appear, from the Western Highlands to the South of England. They like damp woods, or sheltered places on a lawn under trees. Though their bells are mainly white, the inner petals are tipped with green, and the outer petals are green-

backed. On heaths, the gorse flowers on, the yellow blossoms surviving the worst of weathers. Under stones, earwigs are laying their white eggs; when you lift the stone, the male will run off, but the female will stay there motionless, on guard, often lifting her antennae with a protective air.

BRENT geese from Siberia winter in great numbers on the east-coast estuaries and in the Channel harbours. They are stocky, brisk birds, smaller than the other geese, and black and slaty in colour. They prefer to feed on the long-leaved eelgrass that is exposed on the mud at low tide, but in years when they are abundant they are liable to come into fields and eat the winter wheat. Their sharp, barking cry comes loud and clear over the water. Kittiwakes, slim silvery gulls that normally stay well out to sea, are found inland after severe weather; a few are recorded in London in most Januaries. Dippers stay all the winter in their territories on fast-flowing streams; on a sunny day, even at this time of the year, they will sometimes emit their rippling song from a rock overhanging the water. Kingfishers are less faithful to their placid rivers and will move to the coast when conditions are bad.

On horse chestnut trees, the sticky buds are growing fat. On ash trees, the black buds are conspicuous on the grey twigs, the large bud at the tip looking like a pair of tweezers.

IN snow, the tracks of animals and birds leave a record not to be seen at any other time. Rabbits leave the most distinctive marks: a T-shape, consisting of a pair of round prints side by side, followed by two other prints one behind the other. The pair that are side by side are the front tracks, but they are made by the hind legs, since the rabbit when running swings its hind legs in front of its forepaws. A fox trots along more neatly, leaving a straight line of rather confused prints, since its hind feet each fall into the marks left by its front paws.

Birds' tracks show more clearly in shallow snow; a mosaic of prints quickly surrounds a doorstep where food has been thrown down. If a crow has come down it is easy to pick out: it leaves three front toe prints and a thickly padded print from its hind toe, with a long scratch between the prints where it has dragged its feet.

But in the prolonged cold, small birds suffer badly. If they cannot wash their feathers, they stick together, and can no longer be puffed up to insulate them against the frost. Wrens gather in nest-boxes to find warmth at night, as many as forty together, but in the morning the box is sometimes full of corpses. Birds living in marshes and reed beds are also hard hit. Snipe die with their legs frozen together, herons with their beaks clamped shut by ice. Mallard and tufted duck, their feet frozen into the ice of a pond, may be killed there by foxes.

THE birds that survive a cold spell quickly recover — and luckily they are the majority. The dawn chorus is steadily growing stronger, with more and more song thrushes, mistle thrushes and robins joining in. This week the first chaffinches should be heard, some of them only producing the opening notes of their song in the first few days. All the titmice are singing now: the blue tit is the commonest in Britain, and the great tit not far behind in numbers, but the less familiar coal tit is probably as numerous as the great tit. It is found more often in

conifer plantations than in mixed woods and gardens; its song is a quick, vigorous trill, like bubbling water.

Herons are beginning to gather round their old nests; the males utter a loud, honking pairing-call, and point their bills at the sky when a female shows interest. Among the flocks of black-headed gulls, more and more can be seen with their dark brown hood almost complete.

Other survivors are the dry, brown leaves on some young oak trees, which have survived all the assaults of the frost and snow. They will only be pushed off when the new leaf-buds begin to swell.

THE skylarks now singing over the fields are resident birds, but a complicated pattern of skylark migration is also beginning. Some birds that came here from northern Europe in the autumn are starting to drift back across the North Sea, while others are returning to England across the Channel from a winter spent in the south of Europe. Woodlarks are also in song, but they are now rare birds in Britain, with probably only about a hundred pairs remaining on heaths in the South-west and Wales. At the tide-line on some parts of the east coast, shorelarks gather to feed among the seaweed, very distinctive with their black and yellow faces.

Early leaves are showing: there are small shoots on the wild honeysuckle, and here and there on elder trees. By damp ditches, the first delicate leaves of cow parsley are spreading, and the young goose-grass is sticky to the touch. Hazel twigs glow pink in the sunshine: their pale yellow catkins and the tiny red stars of their female flowers are forming. Hazel is now generally known as a shrub, but in Scotland a few large, gnarled trees are found, perhaps similar to the hazel's ancestors.

FIRST blackbirds are singing, from low boughs and chimney pots at sunset. Yellowhammers begin to be heard along country roads, their head and breast brilliant yellow in their spring plumage. Robins are forming into pairs: the females have abandoned their own territories, and each flits back persistently into the territory of a chosen male until he accepts her and lets her stay unharried. He will go on defending the territory, by fighting and posturing, against all other robin invaders.

In Scotland and the Breckland, crossbills are starting to nest on the edge of pine woods. The male is brick-red, the female green; he keeps her company as she builds the stout platform of pine-twigs where she will soon be laying. When they stop to feed, they often hang upside down to get at the pine-cones.

Alder catkins swing on the trees, a dappled red and yellow, side by side with the purple, egg-shaped female catkins, and the old seed-cones from last year. On the lime trees, the buds are red, the twigs pink and olive. Colt's-foot is appearing on bare stretches of roadside: the yellow heads face the sky on their stiff, scaly stems. The colt's-foot leaves only emerge, flat on the ground, after the flowers are out.

In the woods, winter aconites, the earliest to bloom of the buttercup family, display their yellow flowerheads with a ruff of leaves below: they are a southern European flower that has gone native in Britain. On woodland banks, blue flowers are opening on the tough, trailing stems of the periwinkle. Female mosquitoes emerge from hibernation to lay their eggs on stagnant pools; the males died last autumn. It is only the females who bite men and birds.

MAGPIES gather in chattering flocks in the tree-tops, their long tails pointing in all directions. These assemblies seem to express some early spring sexual excitement, before nest-building begins next month. Over lakes and ponds, mallards fly up and down in quacking pairs. Green woodpeckers call with a longer, shriller laugh, the equivalent of song for them. But as ground-feeders, depending very much on ants, their numbers always suffer in the winter frosts. Tree-creepers begin to sing: a few wispy notes, ending in a flourish, uttered as they make their way up a tree-trunk.

Foxes are mating: their chilling screams echo through the night. They are slowly becoming town animals, feeding out of dustbins and making their earths in neglected gardens. Rabbits have begun to breed, and the first litters are being born in their underground nests. The young will be up and out on the grass in a fortnight.

On the hawthorn hedges, the buds are like pale green buttons, and in some places have burst into leaf. On hedge-banks, the buttery-looking stars of the lesser celandine are appearing. On waste ground, the toothed leaves of dandelions grow longer, and young nettles sting the unwary.

SIGNS of spring are multiplying daily. Titmice are busily exploring nesting sites. Blue tits dart in and out of cracks in trees, lamp-posts and hollow pipes; great tits, needing more space, usually control the nest-boxes. Rooks stay longer in the rookeries before setting out to forage in the morning. Ravens are building their bulky nests in high branches and on cliff-ledges. Curlew drift up the west coast of England towards their breeding sites; many have spent the winter in Ireland. Great crested grebes are returning from the coast to lakes and ponds. In London, common gulls are dotted more numerously among the flocks of black-headed gulls, also heading slowly northwards; they are slightly larger than the black-headed gulls, with green bills and legs.

Peacock butterflies and small tortoiseshells are venturing out of hibernation, and looking, along with bumble bees and honey bees, for early flowers. At the edge of woods the first of the sweet violets, the only scented wild violets in this country, are showing through. Some are purple, some are white; lilac, pink or even yellow individuals can occasionally be found.

MORE birds are coming into song. Greenfinches sing from treetops, a rapid twitter leading into a trill of richer notes. Later in the spring they will use the same song in a slow, butterfly-like display flight. Goldfinches are also singing, a breezy, tinkling note, as often on the wing as from a bush. Meadow pipits rise steeply from the grass with a thin call, then glide rapidly down again with a melodious outburst.

Early blackbirds often warble softly to themselves on the ground, their yellow beaks hardly opening at all. They are very active in defence of their territories now. A cock will fly swiftly at an intruder, but as it comes to the edge of its territory it will land and go into a threat display, with beak lifted high, and tail fanned and lowered. Occasionally there is a real fight, with both birds fluttering up into the air and trying to peck each other.

The leaves of the wild arum, or cuckoo-pint, are showing through by the hedges: sharp green spikes that will unfurl to an arrow shape. Elderberry leaves are thick and silky on some bushes, already hiding the pithy grey stems that snap in two so easily. The bare elm trees seem, from a distance, to have a pink or purplish haze around them — it is the massed effect of their tiny red flowers. The first sprigs of 'palm' or 'pussy willow' are ready to pick. They are the catkins of the sallow, or goat willow — the gold catkins are male, the silver ones female. Bees and moths already begin to cluster on them; and at dusk a long-eared bat, just out of hibernation, can sometimes be seen swooping like a hawk over the sallows to catch the insects.

HOUSE sparrows are singing everywhere, though the song is scarcely noticeable as it is no more than a gurgled string of ordinary chirps. Tree sparrows are still in their winter flocks on farmland, and few have yet returned to the orchard trees and pollard willows in whose holes they will nest. Goldcrests break into song like a wheel softly spinning, in the depths of yews and fir trees. They have become much more common in Britain since they invaded the new conifer plantations. Firecrests have established themselves as regular breeding birds in southern England in recent years, particularly favouring Buckinghamshire.

Aspen trees are thick and woolly with catkins, the male ones a rich red, the female long and green. The yellow-green flowers of dog's mercury are abundant on woodland floors: it is one of the only flowers ever to be seen in the barren brown spaces under beech trees. By riversides, the pink clusters of butterbur are coming out, though their leaves, which will grow up to a yard wide, have hardly begun to appear. On rubbish tips, tough old stems of scentless mayweed which survived the winter are putting out white blooms.

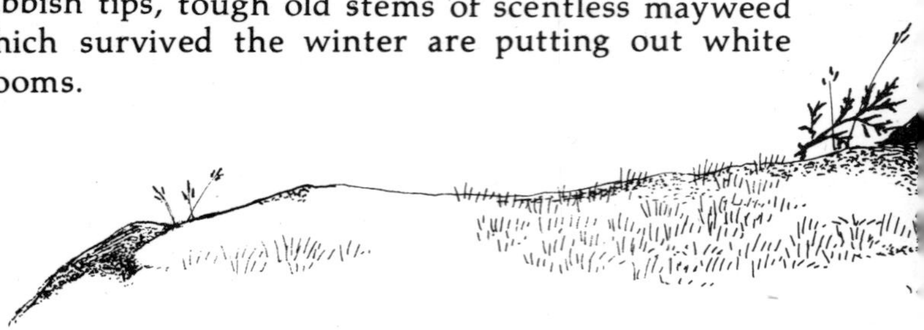

LONG-TAILED tits are building their oval nests in the sprouting hawthorn bushes. Both of the pair bring the moss, and the feathers for the lining; they mutter sharply to themselves as they flit awkwardly along. Lapwings are back over the fields where they will breed; the males wheel and dive, calling loudly, then run rapidly along the ground with their crest held high. Collared doves are singing again: three brisk coos, with the emphasis distinctly on the middle one. Redwings gather in the tree-tops before their departure for Scandinavia, and keep up a fluty, babbling chorus.

Frogs are mating, clamped together in the water, often in large gatherings. The spawn will settle on the bottom of the pond, then float to the top again in jelly-like masses as it absorbs water. Long catkins wave on the high branches of the Lombardy poplars, but female flowers are rare, since most of the British trees are male, propagated from cuttings. Primroses are appearing in woods and on railway embankments; marsh marigolds or kingcups, upright and handsome, bloom along streams, often in the water itself; while on roadsides the first yellow buds of the stubby Oxford ragwort are opening.

19 March – 25 March

THE nesting season is under way. Some herons are already sitting on eggs, in their bulky nests. Both sexes incubate: they greet each other with a cere-

monial flexing of their long necks when one takes over from the other. Song thrushes are building in the bare hedges; they usually lose the eggs from these early nests, either to boys or jays, but soon build again. Mistle thrushes have already laid, in their nests high in the forks of branches. Only the hen sits; the males are singing loudly now in treetops nearby.

The drumming of the great spotted woodpecker rings out in the woods: a territorial defence call, like the songs of other birds. The woodpecker chooses a resonant spot on a dead bough, and hammers at it with its beak at the rate of ten blows a second. Sometimes it does the same thing on the lead at the top of a radio mast. The sound carries up to a quarter of a mile on a still day. Lesser spotted woodpeckers — small black-and-white birds, no bigger than a great tit — drum almost as loudly, though with a higher frequency, of twelve to fourteen blows a second.

Horse chestnut buds are breaking, shedding their sticky brown scales. Wild daffodils, or Lent lilies, are flowering in wet meadows in the South-west and the Lake District; escaped garden daffodils are common on roadsides. Wood anemones are opening in oak woods and hazel coppices — pale white flowers with a faint pink blush. Adders stretch out in the sunshine by the sides of hedges; they will soon go down to the marshlands where they breed. Ladybirds are on the wing again: the two-spot ladybird is the one most often seen in gardens and houses.

THE first summer visitors are back. Chiffchaffs sing in the tops of tall trees, some on their way to their breeding territories, some already in them. Wheatears appear on the downs: they drop off a fence or wall with a flash of their white rumps. Common sandpipers are seen on western coasts, skimming along the water's edge with hesitant, flickering wingbeat. Snipe are 'drumming' over the marshes. For many years, this ringing tremolo was thought to be a vocal sound; in fact it is made by the

two outer tail-feathers and the quivering wings, as the snipe dives through the air. Blackbirds and hedge-sparrows are beginning to build, but eggs are still rare.

Weeping willows are green; on the blackthorn twigs, flower-buds and leaf-buds sit side by side, waiting to open. Red dead-nettles are thick on the ground, dandelion flowers are big and bright. Colt's-foot is in full bloom, and its arrow-shaped leaves are now pushing up through the grass. Dock leaves are spreading, dark green around a pale purple centre. In sunny glades and walks, brimstone butterflies career along with fast, unsteady flight: they have just emerged from hibernation among the ivy leaves.

THE next wave of summer migrants has arrived. Willow warblers are back in the birch trees, repeating their tiny cascades of song again and again. Sand martins flit over the surfaces of the water in flooded gravel-pits. On farms, yellow wagtails dart for insects among the spring grass, and the first few swallows circle round the barns. In the West Country, ring-ousels — like blackbirds with a white bib — make their way back to their breeding haunts on the moors and hillsides. The male golden plovers that are heading north have reassumed their summer plumage, a glittering yellow back and black breast.

Round the bare twigs of the wych elms there are bright green circles of new seeds. On Norway maples, the flowers are appearing before the leaves, in thick yellow clusters bursting from the bud. Pink flowers coat the evergreen branches of Lawson's cypress, and the first open leaves on the horse chestnuts are like small green stars. Dog violets are thick on the banks, larger than the sweet violets but without their scent. Comma butterflies sun themselves in windless gardens: their ragged-looking wings are like dead leaves when closed, apart from the white comma-mark on the underside.

ROBINS are nesting in hedge-banks, or behind the loose bark of trees. They sit tight when discovered, watching the intruder with a shining black eye, and slipping off the nest only at the last moment of safety. Blackbirds are sitting: their grass-lined

nests can be distinguished at a touch from the bare mud bowls of the song-thrushes. Hedge-sparrows, though inconspicuous birds in their soft plumage of browns and greys, are sitting on vivid sky-blue eggs in their mossy nests. Magpies are building: with their long tail, short wings and a long stick in their beak, they look like flying crosses of Lorraine. They roof their domed nests with particularly thorny twigs.

New bird arrivals include blackcaps, whose rich song is often mistaken for the later nightingale's; redstarts, their scarlet tails gleaming as they dip over the dead bracken; and sedge warblers, who keep up a rapid flow of sweet and harsh notes as they flit through the reeds and osiers. Swallows become a common sight. First cuckoos approach the British Isles.

Cowslips open in the meadows, golden flowers with five red spots. In shadowy places, the pale white wood-sorrel stands daintily among its sharply-folded leaves. Rowan trees are speckled finely with green; the young hornbeam leaves are like small spikes. Catkins wave among the new foliage on the birches. Among the early moths are orange underwings, who often fly at this season round the tops of birches; and spring ushers, small moths with thin black markings, who sit on the dead leaves that still linger on oak trees.

WHITETHROATS are back, fluttering above hedges like clumsy skylarks and singing a scratchy song, then dropping down into the leaves. Their numbers declined heavily about ten years ago, but they are becoming commoner again. Black redstarts have returned to their city haunts — derelict buildings and shunting-yards. They sing in short bursts, melodious but hectic, often on high lamps and rooftops. Kestrels have also become city birds. They swoop almost vertically up to the ledges of tall buildings, where they lay their eggs with no pretence at building a nest. Coots fight on the banks of ponds and lakes, often rushing out on to roads in their excitement, under the wheels of cars.

Many horse chestnuts are in full leaf, with their flower spikes also growing rapidly. The young leaves of the Lombardy poplars are more yellow than green, giving a line of the trees an oddly autumnal air. The first bluebells are growing in patches in the woods, where the early bracken is uncoiling; lady's smock, or cuckoo flower, is abundant in wet fields. The small white butterfly is seen again. It is the first species of the year to emerge from the chrysalis state, and not from hibernation like the brimstones and peacocks.

MORE summer visitors are arriving from Africa. Garden warblers sing quietly in woods and parks, grasshopper warblers deliver their high, monotonous trill from deep undergrowth. House martins wheel round the eaves again: their call is like the clicker that lecturers used to employ as a signal to change the slide. The first summer migrants to start

nesting are the chiffchaffs. They are easy to notice, since they call constantly as they approach the brambles where they are building — unlike the willow warblers which have an almost identical alarm call, but only use it when feeding their young.

Starlings are building their big ragged nests in holes and drainpipes; many of their winter companions in the English fields are now back in Russia and Poland, beginning to do the same. A few wintering fieldfares still linger on the east coast.

Dusty red blossoms surround the ash buds, but the leaves have yet to open. Oak buds are just breaking; the pale green leaves of the limes are slightly more advanced. Field speedwells spread in the grass; bluebells begin to cover the woodland floors with brilliant sheets of colour; the cuckoo-pint unfurls its hooded purple spike. The flowers of the colt's-foot have already turned into fat white seed-clocks.

NIGHTINGALES are singing again in thick coppices; spotted flycatchers are back on gates and walls, darting out for insects. Wood warblers have returned to the beech tops; they have two songs, a run of deep notes almost like a nightingale's, and a high shivery trill. Linnets are nesting in gorse bushes; the male twitters excitedly on a high spray, while the female goes deep into the bush with grass and feathers. Stonechats also nest in gorse; they are most commonly found in open land along the coast.

Reed buntings build in osiers and grassy tussocks: they weave their nest of bents, decorating it sometimes with reed-flowers. Nuthatches use mud to plaster up ragged holes in tree-trunks, leaving only a small round entrance; inside they line their nests with flakes of pine bark. Mallard ducklings are already hatched and out on the water, often in broods of nine or ten: they break formation for a moment, then paddle wildly back into a tight cluster again.

Beeches and ash trees are coming slowly into leaf; sycamores are in full leaf, with long, trailing yellow flowers. The first blossom is opening on the hawthorns. Buttercups appear: the tall meadow buttercup in wet fields, the shorter bulbous buttercup more often among the grass on limestone slopes. The glow of the orange pollen is reflected in their shiny yellow petals. Herb-robert is pink on the roadsides. The long stems of ribwort plantain stand high above the grass. Pale water crowfoot is flowering above the surface of streams and ponds. New butterflies on the wing are the orange-tips, especially in meadows where lady's smock is growing; hoverflies hang motionless before the early flowers of the cow parsley.

THE last summer visitors have arrived. Swifts speed through the sky in screaming groups, then swerve up under the eaves. The double purr of the turtle dove comes from thick hedges, like a soft telephone ringing. The rattling song of the lesser whitethroat is heard again on country roadsides; the species is also becoming commoner in town parks, as it is on the Continent. On gorsy heaths, the first whinchats flick their wings and tail, and sing a brief song. With some resident birds, breeding is well advanced: young blackbirds and song thrushes are hopping under bushes, calling out to be fed; while

greenfinches, goldfinches and chaffinches can all be found sitting on eggs in their well-woven nests.

Last of all the trees, the London planes are coming into leaf. There are pink-tipped flowers on the crab-apples, and the sweet-smelling white buds on the rowans will soon open. Pink and white clover are found among the grass and the tiny flowers of the wild forget-me-not along the edge of fields. Wood-ruff sparkles in damp places under the trees. Speckled wood butterflies gather in places where the broken sunlight matches the pattern of their wings.

UNDER the roofs, young starlings keep up an insistent, churring call for food. But young robins in the nest are silent, except when they are being fed: then they produce a thin, vibrant hiss. On lakes and ponds, great crested grebes and little grebes are building their nests — shallow mats of reed, often under overhanging trees. The little grebe, or dabchick, has a loud, whinnying call; its larger relative threatens and courts with softer clicks and trills. Common sandpipers are back by moorland streams; the males fly high in sweeping circles, singing a piping song.

Hawthorn and chestnut trees are laden with white or pink blossom, and the flowers of the whitebeam are opening among its pale leaves. Norway maples already have winged purple seeds, while field maples in the hedge are only just in leaf. The greater stitchwort grows in white masses by the edge of footpaths; scarlet pimpernel flares on waste ground; early purple orchid lifts its fine head above spotted leaves in the meadows. House-crickets, less common indoors than they used to be, sing during warm nights on rubbish-dumps.

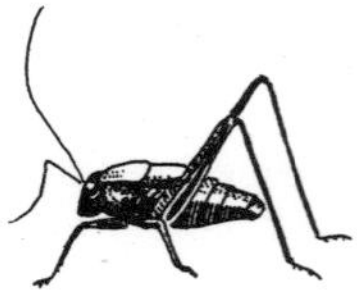

MOST birds are nesting. The males sing strongly at first light, but soon leave their song-posts to help the hen with building, incubating or feeding young. Only a few bachelor males sing on all day. But male cuckoos call constantly, while the hen spends her time watching other birds building, mainly hedge-sparrows and meadow pipits. She will replace an egg of theirs with one of her own in due course. House martins begin to collect mud from the edges of ponds and puddles for their hanging nests under the eaves. Bullfinches start feeding on the dandelion clocks that are standing tall everywhere.

Trees are at their most beautiful, in full leaf but still in the fresh green of spring. In a week or two, they will start to grow darker. Cow parsley, shoulder high, turns the roadsides white. The short-stemmed Oxford ragwort flourishes on even the smallest of waste patches. Yellow tormentil dots the grass. It is the only common flower of the rose family to have four petals. Silverweed, very similar but with the usual five petals, spreads glittering leaves in damper spots. Small heath butterflies flit in groups over the meadows; gnats dance in long columns in the air.

SWALLOWS are building on the rafters of barns and outhouses. They swoop through a low door into the dark space with perfect confidence, but sometimes when they begin building they mistake the rafters, and start two or three different nests side by side. Corn buntings deliver their jangling song from telephone wires; the males often have two or three mates, with nests in widely separated clumps of thistle or weeds. Nightjars sing in the evening, a thin continuous whirr like a sewing-machine, among bracken and low pines; they clap their wings in the air as a mating display at dusk.

Hawthorn flowers turn pink as they fade; and the elders, the white hedgerow flowers of June, begin to display their large rosettes. Flower-buds wait to open on the lime trees. Red campion is thick among the tall grass; the small dandelion-like heads of the smooth hawk's-beard open on their long stems. Broad-leaved willow-herb is in flower; the leaves of its larger and commoner relatives, the rose-bay willow-herb and the great hairy willow-herb, are pushing up steadily.

GULLS' eggs have hatched and the gull colonies are full of downy chicks. Black-headed gulls nest in thousands by inland marshes and pools, as well as on coastal sand-dunes. Herring gulls nest mainly on cliffs, but also on the roofs of houses in seaside towns; the nestlings call with a tremulous whistle, and peck at the red spot on their parent's beak to make them disgorge food. Kittiwakes nest on cliffs and sometimes on window ledges; they are the most graceful but also the noisiest of the gulls, constantly calling with a cry that is accurately imitated in their name.

Terns, being summer visitors, are not so far advanced: they are still hollowing out nests in the sand, or laying their first pebbly-looking eggs. Common and arctic terns are found in mixed colonies in many places on the coast, and some common terns inland at gravel pits. The arctic tern has a more luminous, blood-red bill, with no black at the tip; apart from that, it is almost impossible to distinguish from the common tern. Little terns, daintiest of the family, have been driven from many of their old seaside nesting sites by the spread of bungalows: something under two thousand pairs now nest in small colonies around Britain.

June flowers are already abundant. Foxgloves are open on the hedge banks; yellow pimpernel gleams in shady places; hedge bedstraw edges the roadside with fresh white blossom as the cow parsley fades.

Hogweed and hemlock are growing tall; the hemlock is distinctive with its purple-spotted stem. Tiny flowers dot the sticky goose-grass.

Flowering heads of the grasses sway with the wind: soft meadow grass is common in the fields, meadow barley provides children with itchy darts. In ponds, the black tadpoles begin to take on the shape of frogs.

YOUNG birds are everywhere. Lapwings fly with noisy calls round the head of an intruder, trying to lure him away from the chicks crouching in the grass. Young great crested grebes ride on their parents' backs; when the adult dives, the young are left floating. Guillemots force their young to fly by pushing them off the cliff-ledge, or even by picking them up in their beak and dropping them over the sea. Early nesters like blackbirds and song thrushes are beginning second broods, usually building another nest for the new family.

Delicate pink dog roses fill the hedges. Honeysuckle flowers are especially fragrant at dusk; when they first come out they are white, then when pollinated they turn orange. Ox-eye daisies are massed on railway embankments; buttercups dominate the fields. The yellow flowers of meadow vetchling wind among the grasses. By the waterside, the buds of the yellow iris, like sharp arrowheads, are slowly opening. Half-ripe sycamore seeds and young conkers are blown down by the wind, but there are still trails of white flowers on the locust trees. Young shrews are born; their parents climb the tall grasses to feed on insects that are resting at the top.

ON lakes and rivers, small brown cygnets follow their parents. The adult swans snort and hiss, draw back their necks and arch their wings, if the brood seems threatened. Young goldfinches, just out of the nest, sit in a line on a twig; their parents hover and dance over them. From deep in the foliage comes the thin, insistent note of young blue tit families.

Fewer birds are singing: song thrushes and wrens are now the leading voices. The gruff cooing of stock-doves is heard here and there in the woods: they often nest in small colonies where there are many trees with holes in.

Trees are dark, but small leaves continue to open on the sycamores and maples. Aspens murmur in the breeze before the rain. Early bramble flowers are out; convolvulus sprawls over the hedges. Hedge woundwort is common by the roadside, like a dark nettle with beetroot-red flowers. Common blue butterflies feed on the clover in the fields; at night they sleep clustered together, often with three or four clinging to a single blade of grass.

SMALL flocks of starlings, their breeding season over, are returning to communal roosts in the evening. At dusk, woodcocks go 'roding' — flying with slow wing-beats over the treetops with a sharp cry, keeping to exactly the same route every day. The last birds to be seen before dark are the swifts. Sometimes they wheel high into the sky at last light, probably spending the night on the wing. On the

coast, they will often go out to sea at nightfall: they may be helped to keep aloft by rising currents of air above the water. But on cold summer nights, swifts have another habit: they will cling together in dozens on the side of a wall, like bunches of grapes, in order to keep warm.

The flowers of high summer are coming out everywhere. Lime blossom is thick on the trees, and the strong-scented privet flowers are opening (privet is a native English tree, though now seen most commonly in garden hedges). Tall common ragwort is taking the place of the stumpy Oxford ragwort. The first pink spires of rose-bay willow-herb colour the waste land. Woody nightshade appears in the hedges, enchanter's nightshade in the dark corners of

woods. Small blue dragonflies — more correctly known as 'damselflies' — swarm over brackish water, while the emperor dragonfly, with its four-inch span of lacy wings, hawks energetically for insect prey along river-banks and lakesides. Small frogs begin to clamber on to dry land.

CUCKOOS have fallen silent; but their large, solitary offspring, sprawling across the nests of other birds, open their orange gullets wide. They are fed by their foster-parents, and consume as many insects as the whole brood of reed warblers or meadow pipits that they have pushed out of the nest.

Willow warblers and chiffchaffs are still singing brightly, but will soon be drifting away from their territories with their fully-fledged, leaf-green young. Swifts come down from the sky and speed over the newly-cut hayfields, picking up the insects that have been disturbed. Male yellowhammers sing conspicuously on the hedge-tops, while their mates sit on a second clutch of finely-pencilled eggs.

The nutshells are golden on the beech trees. On hedge-banks, pink and purple are the prevailing colours: red campion is at its peak, rose-bay willow-herb grows more abundant every day, knapweed and mallow are opening. On West Country roadsides, the small green bells of the wall pennywort are common, above the round leaves that give it its name. Prickly black caterpillars swarm on nettles; they will soon turn into brown or green chrysalids out of which the autumn crowds of peacock butterflies will come.

LAST blackbirds are singing; they will not be heard in full song again until February. Finches are still singing strongly — linnets, goldfinches, greenfinches, yellowhammers. All are still breeding, second or even third broods, their nests well hidden in the lush foliage of high summer. Titmice have had their single brood; family parties join up and wander through the treetops. Starlings gather in mobs on the lawns, the brown young — still wishing to be dependent — fighting with the adults for food. All this is local movement; now is the one moment of the year almost without bird migration, north or south.

Lime-tree flowers are in full heady fragrance; the white rosettes of the elderberry are turning brown. On aspen trees, the old leaves are very dark, but new leaves keep coming, dappling them with paler green. The haws are hardening on the hawthorn trees, but there are still fresh green leaves at the bough-tips. Thistleheads are bursting into flower; the rose-bay willow-herb spreads its pink rash across city wasteland and field-edge alike. Grasshoppers start their scratchy tune, rubbing their front wings on their back-legs; at night, the elephant hawk-moth is on the wing, looking for the willow-herb.

YOUNG spotted flycatchers are out of the nest and feeding in garden trees; the air is full of their quick movement and the sharp, scolding notes of their parents. Mistle thrush families feed out on the playing fields; the young have a rapid, twittering call, more like a goldfinch than a thrush. Woodpigeon families feed on the grass with them; the juveniles are as big and heavy-moving as their parents, but still lack the white patch and rainbow colours on their necks. Greenfinches pass overhead singing, with a twisting, erratic flight.

Autumn bird migration begins to be noticed. The first southbound wheatears are seen, flying low over playing fields; sand martins gather in flocks round lakes and reservoirs. (Meanwhile house martins are still busy nesting under eaves, families of eight or even ten crowding into the mud nest to roost at night.) The first warblers are moving south: willow warblers and whitethroats appear in unexpected places. On coasts and estuaries, waders are seen in ones and twos, mostly non-breeding birds coming down from the Arctic. They include greenshank, grey plover, knots and common sandpipers.

On the motorway verges, the yellow-headed wild parsnip is growing tall. White clover has replaced buttercups as the common flower of the hayfields. Many of the flowers of the later summer are drier and more wiry than the spring flowers, like the yarrow and knapweed that are now abundant everywhere. Ragwort plants are eaten down to the stalk by the orange-striped caterpillars of the cinnabar moth; the red and black adults fly at dusk.

ON rocky islands along the west coast of Britain, young Manx shearwaters sit in their nesting-burrows, waiting for their parents. The adults are out at sea all day; they gather offshore on the water at sunset, and come in to feed their young on predigested herrings for an hour or two around midnight. Storm-petrels often nest near them, under overhanging boulders. Like the shearwaters, they have only one nestling, and it too must wait till night for its parents to come in from sea to feed it. On the east coast, starlings and lapwings are beginning to arrive from the Continent. Swifts have started to move southwards, especially the young ones, though many are still screaming in the skies at sunset.

Young foxes move about the country with their mothers, who teach them how to hunt. The domed nests of the harvest mouse are common among the corn stalks. On the turkey oaks, the hairy acorn-cups are appearing, though the acorns in them are still minute. Berries are on the rowan trees, some orange, some already red. Maidenhair fern flourishes in the West, in damp caves or on rocks where it is moistened by the sea-spray. Bracken is tall enough to hide children. Mushrooms are discovered in the fields by early risers.

THIS is the most silent moment of the year for birds. Yellowhammers are the strongest singers now, answering each other loud and clear across the valley; a few wrens and linnets are still to be heard. Most birds are feeding quietly with their families, and beginning to moult; the young are acquiring the first bright plumage of adulthood.

On the coast, terns — common, arctic, Sandwich and little — are still fishing, with their full-grown young, around their breeding sites. Razorbills, guillemots and puffins have mostly left their cliffs in the south, but are still to be seen in the north of England and Scotland. Many gannets are still feeding in inshore waters. Kittiwakes move along the coast with the mackerel and herring shoals. Gulls — herring, common, lesser black-backed and greater

black-backed — are beginning to disperse. Black-headed gulls are losing their chocolate-coloured hoods, and spreading widely inland.

The brightly coloured Vanessid butterflies become common; newly-hatched red admirals and painted ladies join the survivors of the spring immigrants who parented them; the first of the small tortoiseshells emerge, the offspring of butterflies that hibernated in Britain last winter. Six-spot burnet moths cluster half-drunk on the thistle heads.

Wild thyme smells sweet on grassy banks and marjoram, with its dappled head of red and pink, grows tall in chalky places. Three kinds of bellflower fill the countryside with purple: the biggest, the nettle-leaved bellflower, stands in swathes in the ditches; clustered bellflower grows in short spikes on hilly fields; while harebells are found almost everywhere, nodding on their delicate stems.

AT the seaside, cormorants are a common sight, standing on buoys or sandbanks. After they have been fishing underwater, they stretch their wings out wide to dry them, sometimes fanning them gently backwards and forwards. From the Irish and Channel ferries, gannets can be seen diving vertically into the sea from up to a hundred feet high. Their young are still in their seaweed nests on rock islands: the parents leave them to starve once they are fully-fledged, and hunger forces them to fly down to the sea. Guillemots and razorbills have left their nesting cliffs, and swim together in small dark flocks. On the Scottish coasts, eider duck feed just offshore, a brilliant white against the grey water.

Tall plants are now at their largest. Burdocks are five feet high, and spread outwards with their enormous, felty leaves; their hard pink flowerheads are turning into the clinging burrs. River banks are dominated by pink-crested bushes of hemp agrimony, and by the great water dock, with its delicate bracelets of red and green seeds. The first blackberries are ready for picking, while gatekeeper butterflies flock on to the bramble bushes that are still in flower.

Young adders are born on dry heaths and hillsides, and young grass snakes emerge from their eggs in manure and rotting vegetation. Hedgehogs produce their blind and helpless litters.

SOME of the smaller birds are starting to sing again. Starlings whistle on rooftops; in garden trees, the 'saw-sharpening' song of the great tit and the musical whisper of the blue tit are heard; goldcrests sing softly from the depths of yew trees, nuthatches call as they cling to tree-trunks.

House sparrows show their deftness on the wing: they hover over flowers where insects are abundant and dive repeatedly to pick them up. Woodpigeons clamber along the thin branches of rowan trees, falling and fluttering as they lean over to eat the orange berries. Waders arriving on the coasts feed in distinctive ways. Greenshank stride steadily forward, their beaks flat in the water, trawling as they go. Curlew probe deep in the underwater mud with their long, curved beaks. Turnstones, just coming in from Scandinavia, toss pebbles in the air with a vigorous jerk of their beaks and eat the sandhoppers hiding beneath.

The golden samphire glows dully on cliffs and seawalls along the southern coasts; sea lavender makes the salt marshes purple; sea bindweed, smaller and pinker than convolvulus, winds through the vegetation along sandy beaches. Of the dandelion tribe, common sowthistle and the larger, pricklier corn sowthistle stand conspicuously at field-edges everywhere. Thistledown begins to float in the air.

Small skipper butterflies flit weakly over the grass tops, looking for burdock and knapweed: wall browns sun themselves on the roadside. Wasps begin to sting humans in greater numbers.

ON the mountains of northern Scotland, ptarmigan are acquiring their autumn dress. It is quite different from both their summer and their winter plumage. In summer, the upper parts are dark brown; now they are a delicate mottled grey. When winter comes, they will turn pure white, so that the whole bird will merge with the snow. Red grouse are forming packs among the heather, the cock birds often joining one pack, the hens another. Black grouse come down from the moorland edge to feed on the stubble. Golden eagles, where they have bred successfully, circle in family parties above the crags.

Ling, or common heather, covers the mountainsides; with it grows the bell heather, with its bigger, purpler flowers. On wetter moors and in bogland the pink cross-leaved heath takes their place. Bees feed in multitudes on these flowers, and make heather honey in their hives and holes. Scraggy, daisy-like flowers common now on waste ground are the mayweed, the corn chamomile, and the sweet-smelling true chamomile, used for making tea. Blackberrying begins in the hedgerows; boys throwing sticks up for conkers find they are still soft and white when opened.

AROUND the farms, swallows are gathering in large numbers on barn roofs and telephone wires as they prepare to leave for southern Africa. Their numbers are increased on the coast by passage-migrants coming through from northern Europe. But some swallows with third broods are still busy feeding young in the nest. Willow warblers and chiff-chaffs resume their song as they drift towards the south coast; there is some evidence that the young males learn their song from this autumn performance by their fathers. A few young birds try a tentative song themselves.

Interesting bird-sightings grow more numerous on the reservoirs and larger lakes. Black terns from the Continent beat up and down the water's edge, more stolidly than other terns. Black-necked grebes swim far out. Migratory duck — so far, mainly wigeon and teal — increase in number.

Roadsides look dry and brown, with the big dead stems of hogweed standing wanly about. Most flowering grasses have turned to seed. Rye grass and the knobbly cock's-foot grass are turning yellow; couch grass is raked up and burned on farms. Flowers still flourish on riverbanks: gipsywort grows tall, with its dainty rings of pale white flowers among nettle-like leaves, while the blue skullcap lurks among thick tufts of foliage. The main brood of peacock butterflies and the big second brood of small tortoiseshells are emerging from their hanging chrysalids, and swarming on the buddleia and the early Michaelmas daisies.

3 September – 9 September

WHEATEARS heading south frequently appear on golf courses, where swallows swoop just in front of players, picking up the insects they have disturbed. Buzzards reappear over farmland; a pair will circle slowly in the sky, half a mile from each other, keeping in touch with sharp, vibrant cries.

On the stubble-fields, a solitary cock pheasant will stalk along with several hens nearby, while partridges feed in coveys of two or three families. Robins are singing again in a subdued, intermittent way; wrens sing indefatigably. Linnets insert a few bars of song among their hectic twitterings.

Yellow patches appear among the lime leaves; conkers are fat on the horse chestnuts. The mauve, cow-faced flowers of Himalayan balsam line the banks of shady rivers; pink purslane decorates the bare edges of damp woods. Red campion is still common everywhere on hedge-banks, often side by side with the tall musk mallow, a softer pink than the common mallow. Fields are full of butterflies in the sunshine — gatekeepers, meadow browns and wall butterflies — but they settle and vanish when the sun goes behind a cloud. Sometimes they will alight on a golf ball, taking it for an ox-eye daisy.

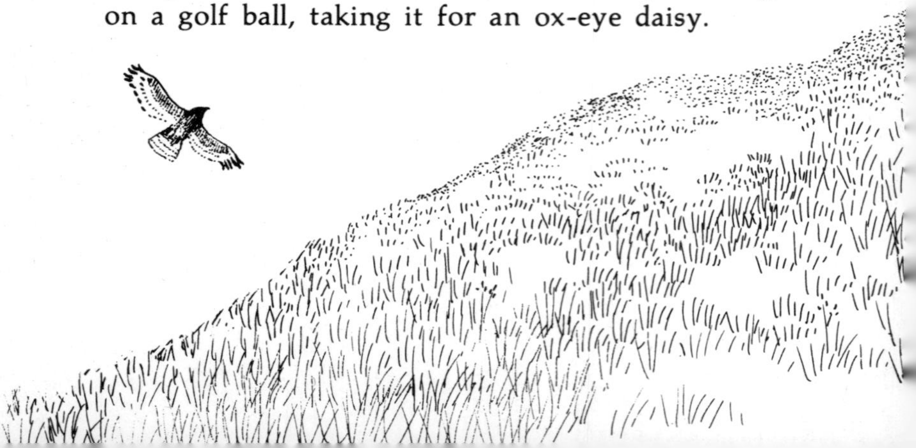

MIGRANTS on the move appear in unexpected places: a whinchat in a garden, a redstart in hawthorn bushes at the edge of a reservoir, yellow wagtails early in the morning by a park pond. But millions of small birds are now passing through England unnoticed, flying high overhead by day or by night, steering by the sun or by the stars. Among resident birds, goldfinches feed in fluttering parties on the downy thistle heads; pied wagtails begin to roost together in large numbers in reed beds and rhododendron clumps; and moulting tufted ducks gather in dull black and white flocks on flooded gravel pits.

Clusters of golden 'keys' hang on the ash trees, contrasting with the still bright green foliage. In moorland lanes, the small, misty-blue flowers of sheep's-bit scabious nestle under the blackberry bushes; the tougher, purple devil's-bit scabious grows on higher land, along with gorse and heather and wild golden rod. Other flowers that go on blossoming into the autumn are the bright yellow tormentil, which keeps close to low, springy grass; and betony, a nettle-like plant with a cluster of crimson flowers at the top.

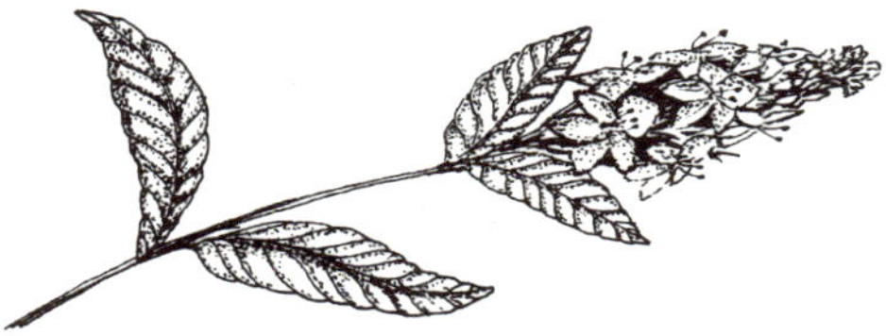

IN the morning mist, fast-flying woodpigeons swerve as they see a human figure looming up. On the dewy grass, large flocks of starlings are feeding, running about energetically but all keeping their distance from each other. Among them are the first winter arrivals from Germany and Poland. Black-headed gulls spread widely inland, their black hoods reduced by now to a dark mark behind the eye; with them there are sometimes lesser black-backed gulls, who will swoop and dive at a dog that disturbs them. Migrating skylarks can often be heard flying low in the mist, as they call musically to keep the flock together.

The fluffy seeds of rose-bay willow-herb whiten waste places. White dead-nettle continues in flower (turned upside down, it reveals a more beautiful and

colourful aspect, with its cross-shaped pattern of four yellow and black anthers). Hornbeams are turning yellow, lime trees are now black and brown. A few oaks have a ring of leaves at their foot. Berries are at their best. On the honeysuckle, they are a brilliant blackish-red; on the guelder-rose, scarlet; on the rowans, bright orange. Blackberries are still to be found, elderberries are steadily being stripped by blackbirds and song-thrushes. Acorns are falling fast, hazel-nuts are pale brown and starting to be picked.

Hawk-moths in different forms are at their most conspicuous: the giant yellow-green caterpillars of the death's head hawk-moth feed on potato leaves, the bright green, pink-striped caterpillars of the privet hawk-moth feed on privet and lilac; while convolvulus hawk-moths, with their four-inch wing-span and five-inch proboscis, fly in from the Mediterranean and feed in English gardens at dusk.

ON the east coast kestrels are coming in from the Continent. They often swoop on other migrating birds — skylarks or linnets — which are resting or feeding on the ground. Out on the sands, southbound waders are at their most numerous now. Dunlin wheel in the sky in flocks of many hundreds — a dark cloud turning to a silver one, as they all turn together and their white breasts catch the sun. Pale sanderling dart through the small breaking waves; knots move steadily across the sand in tightly-packed groups, calling with low grunts and mutterings.

More trees are changing colour; even plane trees, though they will be among the last to fall, are showing a few brown and yellow leaves. Next year's sticky-buds are already developing on the horse chestnut trees; unwary crane-flies get stuck to them as they dance around the twigs. Bracken has turned purple, but other ferns are still green on the hedge-banks — the robust male buckler fern, and the delicate lady fern, whose fronds wither almost as soon as they are picked. Red deer stags are coming down from the moors to join the hinds in the lowland woods, and the annual battle for mates is about to begin.

THE influx of immigrant birds starts to reach new proportions. Starlings arrive in great hordes, some of which will swell the numbers roosting on London buildings. Equally impressive numbers of minute goldcrests make the passage across the North Sea, with skylarks, song thrushes and blackbirds. Larger birds include rooks, jackdaws and herons, and woodpigeons which spread through our woods seeking beechmast. New observation posts for watching these migrants are the oil rigs, where birds wheel around the gas flares in their thousands.

Most trees still look green in sunlight, though on duller days one sees clearly that the leaves are steadily turning. Horse chestnuts and hawthorn join the species which by now have many purple and yellow splashes. Hips and haws shine bright scarlet. Woody nightshade shows its mauve-and-yellow flowers and its red berries on the same hedge, where traveller's joy (or old man's beard) also trails its feathery clusters of seeds. One late brood of butterflies appears: the third brood of the small coppers, which wheel their golden-brown wings over the still-flowering sorrel.

On dewy mornings, spiders' webs make mirrors where the grass is long and tufty.

HERONS still linger round the heronries: on sunny days, they stand on their nests, wings half-spread, warming themselves. They set off to feed by distant lakes and marshes as dusk begins to fall. Starlings are back at their great communal roosts, in thick woods or on city buildings; but some individuals resist the lure of the flock, and sit quietly singing on chimney-pots as the black hordes fly overhead at sunset. Great crested grebes have not

yet left the inland ponds they bred on. The adults have lost the chestnut ruffs they wore in summer, but keep a few black and orange feathers on the sides of their faces; the first-winter birds, still fishing near their parents, have brilliant silvery necks.

Bramblings are arriving in this country now, having deserted the Continental birch forests; they feed under the beech trees, or with chaffinches at the edge of fields. Immigrant siskins spread over southern England, joining up with the lesser redpolls in the tops of alder trees. Of our resident finches, the twite comes down from the northern moors, and settles on salt-marshes and coastal pastures.

On garden walls, ivy-leaved toadflax is still in flower, and the yellow blooms of the ivy itself are full of nectar — the last feeding-place of wasps and hoverflies before they die. Wall-rocket shows bright yellow flowers at the top of stalks from which the long seed-pods stand out like raised arms. Ash-keys are losing their golden glow and turning brown, and sycamore seeds are spinning in flurries to the ground. The crackling leaves at the bottom of hedges are full of life, as slugs and snails go down from the branches and ground beetles hunt for ants and the minute springtails.

Late moths include the angle shades, whose fine green and chestnut markings blend with the dying leaves; and the merveille du jour, whose pale green wings match the lichen on the oak-trunks.

JAYS are busy burying acorns, under leaves or in the cracks in trees. Some of the acorns in the ground will continue to feed them as late as next spring, when they will recognize the new shoots sprouting, and dig them up. Jays are very aggressive at this time of the year, and may be found screaming at a long-eared owl in a spruce wood or a tawny owl in a garden. Chaffinches and greenfinches gather in large flocks in the fields; some of them are continental birds that have just come in: the immigrant chaffinches are pinker round the head than the resident birds. On warm days, goldfinches are singing again.

Geese are back on the Scottish firths and some of the east-coast estuaries. They rest for much of the day and night on sand-bars, or on the water, flighting inland to feed at dusk and dawn. In bright moonlight, they will sometimes stay in the fields all night. The pink-footed geese, the commonest in most places, prefer barley fields; greylag geese stay more on grass. White-fronted geese are also about; more rarely, one hears the ghostly call of barnacle geese.

Many lime trees are almost bare; horse chestnuts look ragged, their leaves sometimes a yellow fringe round a thin green streak; hornbeam leaves wither on the branch, side by side with their hanging clusters of seed. Sycamore leaves turn lemon-yellow; on the Lombardy poplars, the leaves just fade, while the ground beneath is strewn with twigs broken in the wind.

The feathery seeds of old man's beard turn the hedges to clouds. The hard purple heads of knapweed are still to be seen on the roadside. In Scotland, around Exmoor, and in Hampshire the wild red deer stags are rutting. The old stags guard their groups of hinds against the attacks of the young stags; their roars, hoarse and deep, ring through the woods by both day and night, and sometimes they fight with their antlers. Common blue butterflies are still out on the heaths, holly blues in woodland. Female bluebottles try to take up residence in houses, as the days turn colder.

ON blustery days, the black-headed gulls on a ploughed field all sit facing the wind, so that it does not ruffle their feathers. In a light wind, hovering kestrels spread and droop their tails, to give them lift; but in a strong wind they keep aloft without any need to fan their tails. Sometimes they swoop away, letting the wind take them, and start hovering again somewhere else. Small birds are usually silent in the wind; those that do sing — mainly robins, wrens and hedge-sparrows just now — stay in the deep shelter of a bush, and their song is muffled or blown away.

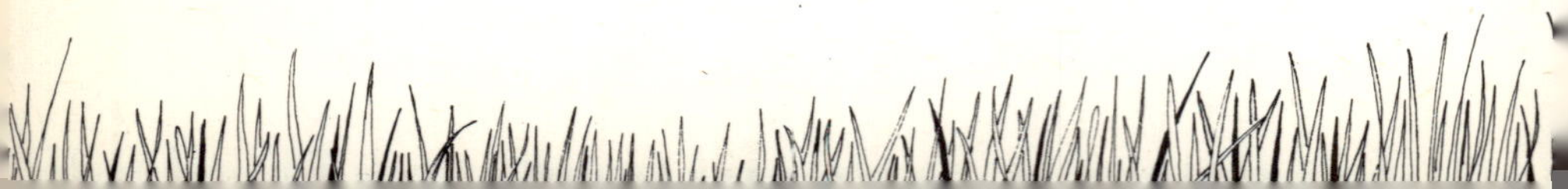

Autumn leaves are mostly in full colour. Beech leaves go from ochre to a fine chocolate colour before dropping; the larch woods are like unbroken sheets of golden flame (it is the only English conifer to shed its needles). Many elder leaves have a pink stain, as if the juice from their own berries has spilt on them. Some hawthorn leaves are a rich claret red. Oaks are withering without making much of a spectacle. On waste patches, the white flowers of scentless mayweed look bedraggled but manage to stand up against the battering of the rain. Escaped Michaelmas daisies are still blossoming in mauve clusters on railway embankments. Ladybirds settle down for winter in the corners of windows.

ON a still night, the sky is sometimes full of the sound of redwings coming down from Scandinavia — a thin, penetrating note that lingers in the air. Fieldfares that have come down with them are more silent on migration, but feeding out on pasture or among the beet, they keep up a loud chatter. Pied wagtails gather on the roofs of tall buildings; they fly from one to another with a deep, looping flight, calling sharply as they rise to the crest of each arc. Song thrushes are singing again in the early morning. In the Scottish Highlands the ptarmigan are assuming their winter plumage of white flecked with brown; and the blue or mountain hare turns white, with black ear-tips. (In both cases the chemical process is the same as the whitening of human hair with age.)

Plane trees are multicoloured, with green, yellow and brown leaves jostling each other. Ash trees and walnuts are still very green. Dormice leave their summer nests and prepare to sleep underground, often surrounded by hazel-nuts stored for mid-winter waking. Voles are making the most of the abundant food: bank voles climb into the hedges for the hips and haws, water voles heap up beechmast in their riverside holes. But in some hedges, as the birds clear the edible fruit, only the poisonous red berries of the black bryony remain.

As the days grow shorter, robins, with their large eyes, are out feeding before dawn. Herring gulls are also early risers; in seaside towns, they swirl over the rooftops with loud wailing cries at the first sign of light. On mild mornings, a faint impulse to build a nest seizes female blackbirds and house-sparrows: they pick up stems of dry grass and fly with them for a distance before dropping them again. Stonechats remain in their territories on coastal heaths: they sit on bare bushes or withered stalks of hemlock, and drop swiftly to the ground for their insect prey.

Wild duck from the Continent are spreading across English inland waters. Many wigeon from Russia

have joined the small breeding population of our own, their loud, whistling yelps ringing over the misty waters on a cold morning. (At close quarters, one sees that they call with a wide open beak.) Pochard come in large numbers to the South of England, especially the Thames Valley, many of them from Germany, some from Scotland. They dive continually, with a quick heave of the shoulders. On land, blackbirds are beginning to be noisy again in the evening, their insistent 'chink, chink, chink' heard for minutes at a time before they settle down to roost in the shrubberies.

Woods and parks look distinctly wintry, though where the leaves still linger they are bright. Especially brilliant are the yellow leaves of the Norwegian maples. Rowan leaves are red, almost like their berries, which have now mostly been eaten by woodpigeons and squirrels. Sweet chestnut leaves are lying thick and yellow under the trees, their prickly pods often hidden beneath them. In beech hedges, the dry orange leaves will stay on the twigs till spring. In damp places, next year's cow parsley is already pushing its leaves up through the grass. Male mosquitoes are dead and the female are hibernating; but harmless winter gnats dance in the air in swarms on a sunny afternoon.

MOST of the small birds that visit Britain in the summer have left; a few last swallows and house martins are leaving, a late chiffchaff still sings. A few blackcaps may stop for the winter in southern England.

Some of the Arctic duck wintering in Britain stay mainly out to sea. Scoters are common now along the south and east coasts. They stay on the water, rarely coming even on to sandbanks, often in big flocks, the drakes a glossy black from bill to tail. Swimming, they stick their tails sharply in the air, like the more elegant and colourful pintails. These are also marine birds, but come inland more often than the scoters; solitary individuals may sometimes be seen in town parks, feeding with the mallard and the tufted ducks. The pintails never dive; when they 'up-end' they depress their pointed tail.

With the cold weather, red squirrels are more sluggish, feeding mainly in a frenzied burst of activity in the early morning. Grey squirrels are as active as ever, frequently invading gardens now. Butterflies cope with the winter in a variety of ways. Some, like the peacocks, hibernate in the winged form. Others, like the white butterflies, pass the winter as chrysalids, while some survive as caterpillars. The caterpillars of the ringlet and the small heath hardly even hibernate; they rest torpid in the long grass, and on days when the sun is warm resume life for another short meal.

RAVENS do not move far from their cliff or crag, whatever the weather. Even though the days are short for feeding, they will pause to play in their flight, briefly gliding upside down or suddenly dropping a hundred feet. Carrion crows also stay around their breeding areas, in pairs or small family parties; on the coast they will sometimes feed now by dropping crabs on to rocks to break the shell. Hooded crows, with their grey backs and chests, are more sociable and restless: thousands have flocked in from the Baltic during the past six weeks and scattered along the shores of southern England.

On the alders, there is a purple glow from the small hard catkins that will soften in the spring. They sit on the twigs side by side with this year's black seed-cones. On many oak trees, the leaves continue to cling, yellow and bony-looking. Oak-apples are falling: they are the dry, empty homes of a tiny wasp, the oak-apple gall. Red, raised patches on the oak leaves are the homes of another wasp, the spangle gall; these, unlike the oak-apples, are still occupied, and the adults will emerge in April. Bracken is purple and brown, but still stands upright, its fronds spread like wings. The small, starry flowers of the shaggy soldier nestle under walls; the last skullcaps hang their blue flowers over riverbanks.

Badgers dig their deep winter quarters, lining the cavity with fallen leaves to give off a musty warmth;

before long, the entrances will be blocked, and the badgers will sleep. Grass snakes hibernate among the tree-roots at the bottom of hedges, often twined together in groups for mutual comfort.

FOR a month or two at the end of the year, mistle thrushes roost in small flocks, settling down at dusk with much churring and clucking in a fir tree or thick hedge. By January they will be roosting in pairs again. On a sunny morning, blackbirds sing a soft, whispering song to themselves in the middle of a bush; the young males, with a dash of brown in their black plumage, can often be heard doing this. Moorhen come ashore to feed on hawthorn berries and crab-apples that are lying on the ground; they step slowly and delicately, but run fast for the water if alarmed.

Two kinds of wild swan are now wintering in Britain. Both are Arctic birds; both have black-and-yellow beaks and tall, straight necks. The whooper swan is commonest in Scotland, especially in the Outer Western Isles; it has a ringing, bugle-like call. Bewick's swan spreads across England; it is a smaller bird, and its notes are more often a musical chatter and murmur. Apart from their cries, both of these swans fly almost silently — unlike our own mute swans, with their booming wing-beats.

Trees show their winter shapes: limes display their zig-zag branches, sycamores reveal the airy spaces between their boughs, hornbeams look like thick brushes (though the young hornbeams hold on to their dead leaves). Only the birches, with their dry catkins and feathery twigs, seem to keep the shape of summer.

WAXWINGS from the Scandinavian forests appear in gardens, particularly where they find the bright red fruit on the cotoneasters: they are rather tame birds of unmistakable appearance, with their swept-back crests and blobs like sealing-wax on their wings. Firecrests from central Europe settle on the south coast of England, often in dead bracken on the downs and cliffs. Tawny owls start hooting more frequently at night; now, especially in the towns, they feed mainly on starlings and sparrows caught at their roosting-places. Great spotted and lesser spotted woodpeckers thrive on the larvae in the dead elms.

In the mountains, some stoats turn white to match the snow; occasionally the change is only partial, leaving brown 'spectacles' round the stoat's eyes. Frogs bury themselves deep in the mud at the bottom of ponds. Most of the flowers still in bloom are humble and inconspicuous — groundsel, chickweed and shepherd's purse — but here and there a dandelion or buttercup remains. Rushes are still erect and pithy at the water's edge; and the leaves of most grasses stay green; though these are the tough old blades of autumn. The fresh green leaves of grass will not be seen till spring.

LARGE, chattering flocks of fieldfares are common now out on the fields or in hawthorn hedges. The redwings that are often found with them are quieter, and less easily alarmed. Our resident thrushes, the song thrush and the mistle thrush, do not mix much with these winter visitors. But both the redwing and the fieldfares have established themselves over the last decade as regular breeders, in small numbers, in Britain. In the woods, treecreepers and goldcrests travel about with the tit flocks. The treecreepers work their way steadily up a tree trunk, then flit down to the base of another tree as the flock moves on, while the goldcrests stay well up among the branches.

Young spruces are cut for Christmas trees; on the older spruces, the seeds ripen slowly, usually taking a year from flowering to the opening of the long, elegant cones. On Scots pines, the cones do not normally drop their seeds till they are two years old. These pine cones are much ravaged by squirrels and woodpeckers, and in Scotland and Norfolk by the crossbills, which wrench them off the branches and hold them in their claws, while extracting the seeds with their tongues.

THREE species of a peculiar family of ducks are among the winter visitors to Britain. These are the 'sawbills' — diving, fish-eating ducks with toothed beaks. Goosanders are quite common on lakes and reservoirs — the drakes with bottle-green heads, black backs and ruddy-white bodies, their mates with rusty red heads. Red-breasted mergansers usually stay on the coast: the drakes are distinguished from the goosanders by their chestnut breasts and notice-

able stiff crests. Both these species sometimes swim with their beaks or even the front of their heads under water, looking out for fish. The third sawbill is a smaller bird, the smew, also quite common on big lakes now: the drake at a distance looks pure white, though through field glasses one can see a black eye and fine black pencilling. These ducks leap up from the water as swiftly as teal.

The only common trees to keep their leaves in the winter, apart from holly and the conifers, are the box and the holm oak. Boxes take strange shapes at human whim in gardens; they are only found in abundance as wild trees on Box Hill in Surrey. Holm oaks are sturdy, shapely trees, resistant to the frost.

IN harsh weather, birds puff their feathers out to keep warmer. But in snow, or with the ground frozen, many find it hard to get food, and mortality is high in prolonged frost. When bread is thrown down, birds quickly gather, but some species are easier to help than others. Robins are tame enough to come into houses, but seem to fear the beaks of hungry starlings and woodpigeons. Blackbirds swoop down and snatch up food quicker than all other birds,

though they waste time in brisk quarrels among themselves. Black-headed gulls flock in from far away and hover deftly, catching in the air any crumb that is thrown to them.

Red berries are plentiful on the holly trees, though much in demand from thrushes and blackbirds. Picking them is easier higher up, since the leaves at grazing height have prickles all round, while leaves at the top have only a single prickly point. Mistletoe flourishes in black poplars and in apple trees, though it is not so common in oaks, in spite of legend. The sticky white berries adhere to birds' bills, especially mistle thrushes', and the seeds get wiped off on the branches of other trees, which the mistletoe then colonizes. Little else is green in the bare woods and orchards, on these days when the sun stays so low.

Index